The Trail of Tears

W9-DFK-213

by Michael Burgan

Content Adviser: Professor Sherry L. Field,
Department of Social Science Education, College of Education,
The University of Georgia

Reading Adviser: Dr. Linda D. Labbo,
Department of Reading Education, College of Education,
The University of Georgia

COMPASS POINT BOOKS

Minneapolis, Minnesota

Compass Point Books
151 Good Counsel Drive
P.O. Box 669
Mankato, MN 56002-0669
877-845-8392
www.capstonepub.com

 This book was manufactured with paper containing at least 10 percent post-consumer waste.

Photographs ©: Woolaroc Museum, Bartlesville, Oklahoma, cover; Archives & Manuscript Division of the Oklahoma Historical Society, neg. #6393, 4; Stock Montage, 5; Archive Photos, 17; The Newberry Library/Stock Montage, 6, 22; XNR Productions, Inc., 7; Cherokee Historical Association, 8; Hulton Getty/Archive Photos, 9, 10, 15, 21, 24 (top), 25, 27, 30 (top), 31; North Wind Picture Archives, 12, 13, 16, 18, 19, 26, 28, 29, 32, 35, 41; Archive Photos, 17; Burstein Collection/Corbis, 23 (left); Stock Montage, 23 (right), 30 bottom, 36; Marilyn "Angel" Wynn, 24 (right); Archives & Manuscript Division of the Oklahoma Historical Society, neg. #1046.B, 33; Library of Congress, 37, 38; William J. Weber/Visuals Unlimited, 39.

Editors: E. Russell Primm and Emily J. Dolbear
Photo Researcher: Svetlana Zhurkina
Photo Selector: Linda S. Koutris
Designer: Bradfordesign, Inc.

Library of Congress Cataloging-in-Publication Data
Burgan, Michael.
   The Trail of Tears / by Michael Burgan.
      p. cm.—(We the people)
   Includes bibliographical references and index.
   ISBN 978-0-7565-0101-3 (library binding)
   ISBN 978-0-7565-0937-8 (paperback)
      1. Trail of Tears, 1838—Juvenile literature. 2. Cherokee Indians—History—Juvenile literature. 3. Cherokee Indians—Relocation—Juvenile literature. I. Title. II. We the people (Compass Point Books)
   E99.C5 B8885 2001
   973'.04975—dc21

                                                                              00-011019

Printed in the United States of America in Stevens Point, Wisconsin.
082011   006324

TABLE OF CONTENTS

THE LONG MARCH

The year was 1838. A long line of Cherokee Indians trudged through the Georgia countryside. These Native Americans were heading for the Indian Territory in Oklahoma. The Cherokee did not choose to make this long, difficult trip. The U.S. government had forced them from their homes and set them on this march of about 800 miles (1,287 kilometers).

The Cherokee's journey west was long and difficult.

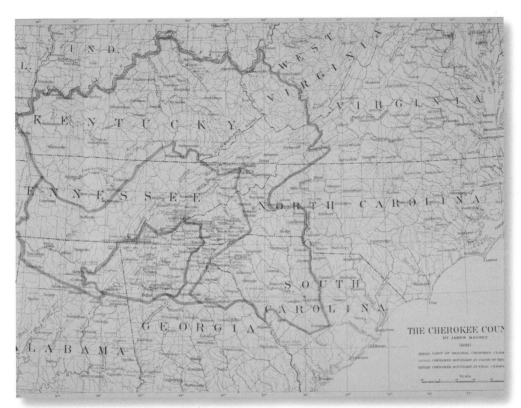

This map shows traditional Cherokee lands.

It was November, and the last of thirteen groups of Cherokee had just left for the Indian Territory. A few Indians traveled by water. Most traveled by land. Women carried their babies in their arms. The sick and elderly bounced along in slow-moving wagons.

*Cherokee leader
John Ross*

George Hicks led one of the Cherokee groups. Before leaving, he sent a letter to John Ross, the leader of the departing Cherokee. Hicks wrote, "It is with sorrow that we are forced by the authority of the white man to quit the scenes of our childhood. We bid a final farewell to it and all we hold dear."

The trip to the Indian Territory took about six months. The Cherokee marched through rain, snow, and bitter cold. Many people died of disease. Many others had died before the trip started after the U.S. government had put them in jail.

In their own language, the Cherokee who survived the march called their route "the trail where they cried." Today it is known as the Trail of Tears.

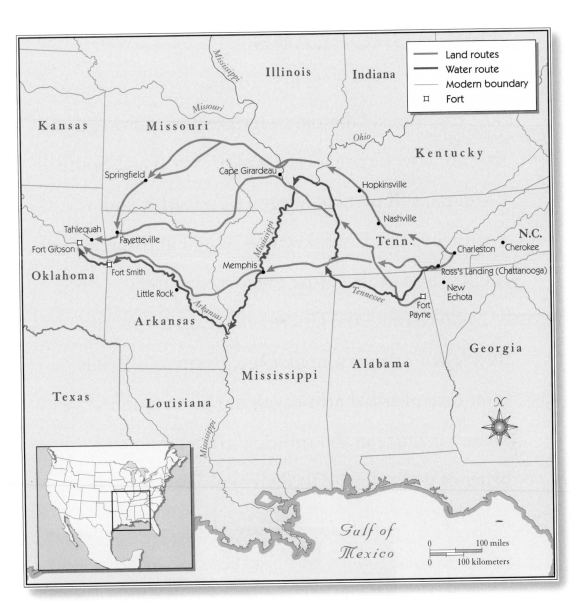

Trail of Tears westward routes

THE EUROPEANS

The traditional Cherokee lands included the regions that are now Georgia, Tennessee, North and South Carolina, and parts of Virginia, Alabama, and Kentucky. The Cherokee had settled in this area hundreds of years before the forced march.

Over time, the Cherokee set up towns and developed a government. One group of officials took care of tribal affairs during peacetime. A second group ran the military affairs. Some of the officials were elected to their positions.

The Cherokee once lived in cabins much like this one.

8

The Spanish explorer Hernando de Soto

Women were important in the culture and served on tribal councils. A Cherokee child's family history was traced through the mother's relatives.

In 1540, the Cherokee encountered their first European—the Spanish explorer Hernando de Soto. De Soto was searching for gold in the southeast region of North America. The explorer never found the gold he was looking for, but he did find some Cherokee Indians—and he shared a meal with them.

During the late 1600s, the Indians traded with the Europeans.

In the second half of the 1600s, Cherokee contact with Europeans increased. French and English traders had joined the Spanish in North America. Traders came to the Cherokee territory seeking furs. In return, the Cherokee received iron tools, guns, and alcohol.

10

Some traders married Cherokee women and stayed to live with the Indians. Some of the sons of white men and Cherokee women adopted European habits. Many old Cherokee customs and religious beliefs slowly began to fade.

During the 1700s, England and France competed for control of North America. For military and economic help, the two countries turned to the various American Indian tribes. At first, the Cherokee supported the French, but the English tried to recruit the Cherokee as allies. These Indians were respected warriors and good trading partners.

During the 1730s, Cherokee chief Attacullaculla visited London, England. He signed an agreement with the English pledging his support. "For though we are red, and you are white," Attacullaculla said, "yet our hands and hearts are joined together."

11

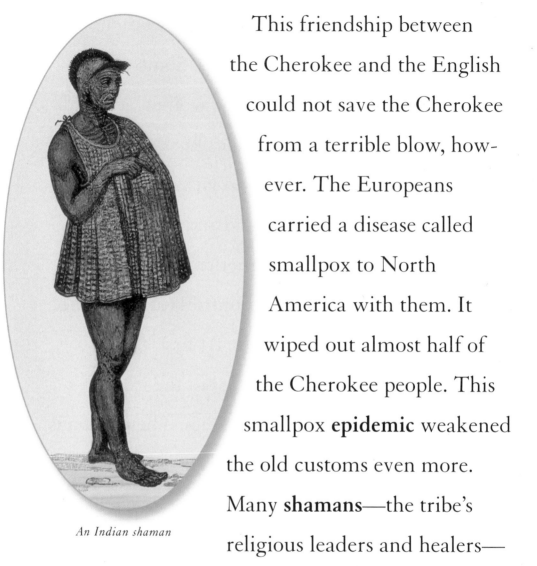

An Indian shaman

This friendship between the Cherokee and the English could not save the Cherokee from a terrible blow, however. The Europeans carried a disease called smallpox to North America with them. It wiped out almost half of the Cherokee people. This smallpox **epidemic** weakened the old customs even more. Many **shamans**—the tribe's religious leaders and healers—lost influence among their people when they could not save their people from the foreign disease.

12

BATTLES AND TREATIES

During the 1750s, France and Great Britain struggled to claim North America, which led to the French and Indian War (1754–1763). At first, the Cherokee fought for the British, but many of the English settlers hated the Cherokee. A massacre of about two dozen Indians took place in Virginia.

Troops destroyed Indian villages.

13

The enraged Cherokee responded by attacking the colonists and capturing a British fort. The British then turned against their former allies, destroying Cherokee towns and farmland.

When the fighting ended, the British used their power to further weaken the Cherokee. New treaties took away Cherokee lands. British influence within the tribe was also growing, as more white men married Cherokee women.

Despite their battles with the British, the Cherokee did not abandon all ties with them. The British offered the Cherokee some protection against the American colonists. The colonists still had bitter feelings about the Cherokee and were eager to take over their lands. When the American Revolution began in 1775, the Cherokee fought with the British against the American colonists.

White men sometimes married Indian women.

A medal given by the British to American Indians who supported them during the American Revolution

Many Cherokee died during the war, and the tribe lost even more land to the Americans.

In 1783, the United States won its independence from Britain. Two years later, a beaten Cherokee people signed its first treaty with the new United States. In the Treaty of Hopewell, the U.S. government set new boundaries for Cherokee lands. The government also pledged that no Americans would settle on these lands. The treaty ended with this promise: "The hatchet shall be forever buried, and the peace given by the United States, and friendship reestablished

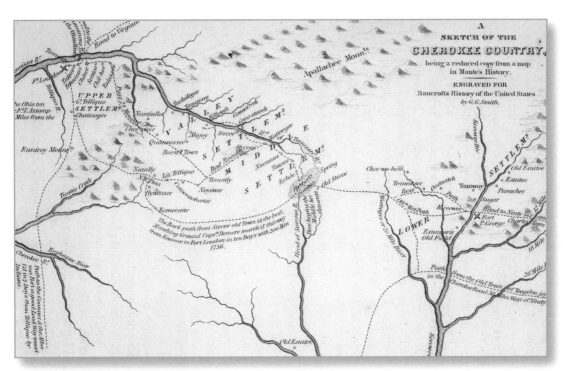

A sketch of the Cherokee lands in the East

between the said states . . . and all the Cherokees . . . shall be universal."

After the Treaty of Hopewell was signed in 1785, fighting still flared between the Cherokee and the American settlers. More treaties followed. They were designed to keep the peace—but they always resulted in the Cherokee giving up more land.

17

Becoming "Civilized"

Under President George Washington, the U.S. government started a policy that dramatically changed the Cherokee way of life. Washington believed that the various American Indian tribes could become U.S. citizens—if they lived more like European Americans.

An Indian woman

In 1792, Congress gave the Cherokee cotton seeds and spinning wheels. Within a year, Cherokee women were growing cotton and spinning it into cloth. At this time, Cherokee men still hunted animals for furs. The women

18

made more money selling cotton than the men did selling furs.

Some of the Cherokee leaders were a mix of white and Cherokee. They encouraged the people in their tribes to adopt more of the white culture.

During the next few years, the Cherokee accepted more spinning equipment and farm tools. They also began raising sheep for wool. A few Cherokee developed **plantations** and became rich. Some bought African-American slaves, as did some white farmers.

The Cherokee took up spinning and other European-American practices.

Many of the Cherokee resisted the changes, however. Some left the Cherokee territory for Arkansas. Cherokee people had moved to Arkansas as early as the 1760s, and small groups continued to settle there. The number grew after 1817. That year, the U.S. government offered the Cherokee land in Arkansas in exchange for their land in the Southeast. The government wanted to open the Cherokee territory to white settlers. America was growing, and people in the East were pushing westward looking for land.

In the tribal homeland, the religious life of the Cherokee was also changing. Members of the Moravian Church, a Protestant religion, set up a school on Cherokee land. Over time, the Moravians taught the Cherokee the religious beliefs of Christians.

Members of other churches also came to **convert** the Indians to Christianity. In 1813, the Cherokee leader Charles Hicks became a Christian, and more Cherokee soon followed.

The American influence affected Cherokee government too. In 1827, the Cherokee drafted a

Missionaries tried to convert American Indians to Christianity.

21

Chief John Ross

constitution that was similar to the U.S. Constitution. The Cherokee document, like the U.S. Constitution, called for three branches of government. In 1828, under the new government, John Ross was elected principal chief of the Cherokee. His government ruled from the capital at New Echota.

Another important development for Native Americans was the introduction of a Cherokee alphabet. No other Indian tribe had a system for writing its language.

In 1821, a Cherokee named Sequoyah created the first written alphabet for an Indian language. In 1828, Elias Boudinot published the

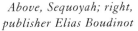

Above, Sequoyah; right, publisher Elias Boudinot

Cherokee Phoenix, America's first Indian newspaper. The paper was printed in English and Cherokee.

The changes in Cherokee culture were also influencing neighboring tribes. The Choctaw, Chickasaw, and Creek were adopting American habits too. Whites sometimes called these three tribes, along with the Cherokee and the Seminole of Florida, the Five Civilized Tribes.

23

Above, a Choctaw camp; right, the Cherokee Phoenix

The Cherokee were considered the most **civilized** Native Americans. Chief John Ross hoped that if the Cherokee accepted American culture, the U.S. government would leave them alone and not take more of their land. His hopes did not last long.

THE RUSH FOR GOLD AND LAND

Andrew Jackson

In 1828, Andrew Jackson was elected the seventh president of the United States. Jackson and the Cherokee had once fought together against the Creek. During one battle, a Cherokee warrior had even saved Jackson's life. Nevertheless, Jackson considered the Indians "savages" and argued that moving them would be for their own good. The new president believed that the American Indians in the East should move west, to the Indian Territory in Oklahoma.

A growing number of Americans wanted to

25

The discovery of gold drew more white people onto Indian lands.

settle the Indian lands of the Southeast. In July 1828, gold was discovered in the Cherokee territory, which made the region even more appealing. White miners quickly staked claims on Cherokee land. The leaders of Georgia wanted control of that land, and Jackson encouraged them. "Build a fire under [the Cherokee]," Jackson said. "When it gets hot enough, they'll move."

In its struggle against the Cherokee, Georgia

had an old law on its side. In 1802, President Thomas Jefferson had signed the Georgia Compact. Under that agreement, Georgia would receive Cherokee lands, and the Cherokee would be removed. Jackson was not going to stop Georgia from trying to take

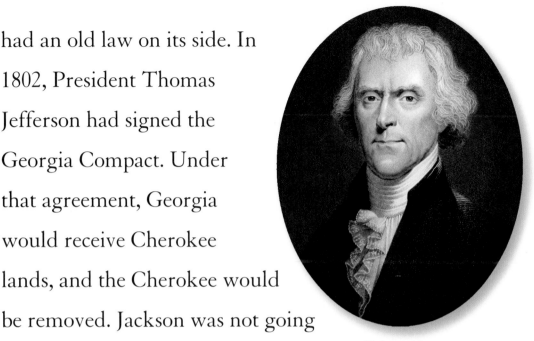

U.S. president Thomas Jefferson

the Cherokee land. President Jackson also proposed the Indian Removal Act, a law that would move all eastern Indians from their native lands.

Congress debated the Indian Removal Act for months. The law was finally passed in May 1830. During this time, Georgia passed a law that took away Cherokee rights. The Indians could not mine gold, or speak in court against a white

27

For months, members of Congress debated the Indian Removal Act.

person, or hold political meetings—unless the purpose of the meeting was to sell their land. In response, the Cherokee made it a crime for any tribal member to sell land to whites. The sentence for any Cherokee who broke this law was death.

As miners poured into their land, some of the Cherokee wanted to fight them off. During one raid, a band of Cherokee burned the houses of white settlers. Most Cherokee leaders realized that they could not beat the Americans in a war, however. Chief John Ross decided that the tribe should fight for its land in the U.S. Supreme Court.

Twice, the Cherokee challenged Georgia's right to pass laws affecting the tribal nation. In the first case, the Court said that it did not have the legal authority to rule in the matter. In the second

The U.S. Supreme Court in the mid-1800s

29

case, decided in 1832, the Court ruled in favor of the Cherokee. Chief Justice John Marshall said that only the U.S. government had the power to pass laws affecting the Cherokee. Georgia's restrictions against the Cherokee were overturned, which means they were no longer lawful.

THE CASE

OF

THE CHEROKEE NATION

against

THE STATE OF GEORGIA:

ARGUED AND DETERMINED AT

THE SUPREME COURT OF THE UNITED STATES,

JANUARY TERM 1831.

WITH

AN APPENDIX,

Containing the Opinion of Chancellor Kent on the Case; the Treaties between the United States and the Cherokee Indians; the Act of Congress of 1802, entitled 'An Act to regulate intercourse with the Indian tribes, &c.'; and the Laws of Georgia relative to the country occupied by the Cherokee Indians, within the boundary of that State.

BY RICHARD PETERS,

COUNSELLOR AT LAW.

Philadelphia:

JOHN GRIGG, 9 NORTH FOURTH STREET.

1831.

Top, Chief Justice John Marshall; right, the title page of the Supreme Court decision about the Cherokee

30

THE FINAL RESISTANCE

Despite the Supreme Court's ruling, however, Georgia continued to take Cherokee land and force the Indians from their homes. President Jackson refused to use his authority to stop Georgia.

Major Ridge

By 1834, some Cherokee leaders felt that their situation was hopeless. A Cherokee leader named Major Ridge, along with his son John and Elias Boudinot, led a group of Cherokee who were ready to sell their lands and move west. They were later known as the Treaty Party, or Ridgists.

31

The U.S. House of Representatives in the mid 1800s

Chief John Ross led a much larger group of Cherokee who wanted to keep fighting for their land. They were sometimes called the Nationalists. In 1835, both groups met with U.S. representatives in Washington, D.C. The Treaty Party made a deal to sell the Cherokee land in return for land in Oklahoma and $4.5 million.

Ridge returned to Georgia to present the new treaty. President Jackson soon sent a letter to the

Cherokee, encouraging them to accept the deal. The president wrote, "You cannot drive back the laws of Georgia from among you. Every year will increase your difficulties." By now, most of the other Indian tribes in the region had accepted similar deals and were moving west. Most Cherokee sided with Ross, however, and opposed Ridge's treaty.

The Cherokee delegation to Washington, D.C.

33

In October 1835, the Cherokee met to discuss the treaty. The majority voted against it. In December, Ross returned to Washington to try to work out a new deal.

Ridge stayed behind and held another meeting to debate the treaty. Only about eighty people at the meeting were legally able to vote, and the Ridgists were the most important leaders present, so Major Ridge got his way. The Treaty of New Echota was approved in December.

Ross ordered the Cherokee to ignore the treaty, which opposed the wishes of most of the tribe. Meanwhile, about 7,000 U.S. troops arrived to protect the members of the Treaty Party. Jackson hoped the troops would frighten the Indians and discourage Cherokee opposition to the treaty.

Ross still hoped to prevent the removal of the

Chief Ross wrote that the decision to relocate his people stripped them of all dignity.

Indians from their land. After the U.S. Senate approved the treaty, he fought to have it reversed. In September 1836, he wrote a letter to U.S. political leaders. Because of the Treaty of New Echota, Ross argued, "We are stripped of every **attribute** of freedom. . . . Our property may be plundered before our eyes; violence may be committed on our person; even our lives may be taken away. . . . We are deprived of membership in the human family!" The government ignored Ross's pleas.

BEFORE THE MARCH

In January 1838, the first Treaty Party members left Georgia. Under the treaty, the Cherokee had two years to prepare for removal, and that time had almost passed. In May 1838, General Winfield Scott

General Winfield Scott

arrived in New Echota to organize the removal of Ross's people. He commanded a force of 7,000. State **militia** from Georgia and Tennessee also took part.

The soldiers' first job was to put the Cherokee in **stockades**—small, enclosed forts used as prisons. Some Cherokee willingly left their land. Others were forced off by soldiers wielding bayonets and were not allowed time to collect their

36

property. General Scott ordered the U.S. troops to treat the Cherokee well, but the state militia was more ruthless. One observer described how soldiers "drove [200 Cherokee] through the Chickamauga River before them like cattle. . . . It was pitiful to see the poor folks, many old and sick . . . and all utterly exhausted."

The Cherokee in the stockades had to live in cramped, dirty quarters. Some soldiers took the Indians' food and sold it to local people. Disease was everywhere, and women and children were abused. One Georgia guard later wrote, "The Cherokee removal was the cruelest work I ever knew."

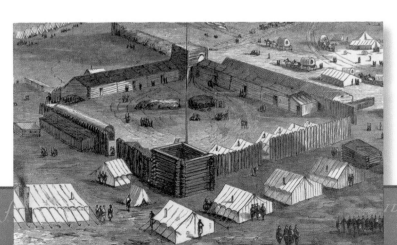

A typical military stockade

THE TRAIL OF TEARS

In June, the first Cherokee left the stockades for the Indian Territory in Oklahoma. They set off by barge along a river route. The summer heat and disease killed many of the travelers. Cherokee leaders

General Scott led the westward march.

asked Scott to delay the rest of the removal until autumn, and he agreed. Ross also convinced Scott to let the Cherokee themselves organize the march.

The removal began again in October. From then on, the Cherokee traveled mostly by land. Disease and harsh weather killed many, especially the very young and old. One soldier who traveled with Ross's group described a terrible sleet and snowstorm. He noted that many Cherokee "had to sleep in the wagons and on the ground without fire." A traveler

The image on this monument honoring Indians is also on the Oklahoma state flag.

from Maine, who came upon some Cherokee camped in a forest, wrote, "We learned . . . that they buried fourteen or fifteen at every stopping place."

By the end of March 1839, the last of the Cherokee Indians reached Oklahoma. About 17,000 members of the tribe had been forced from their land. As many as 4,000 were dead. About one-third of these deaths occurred in the stockades. John Ross's wife, Quatie, was one of those who died. She was buried in Little Rock, Arkansas.

Graves of other fallen Cherokee marked the route that the Indians marched along—which came to be known as the Trail of Tears. An elderly Cherokee recalled that, during the march, "children cry and many men cry, and all look sad when friends die, but they say nothing and just put [their] heads down and keep on going West."

In Oklahoma, Chief John Ross once again served as the Cherokee leader. The leaders of the Treaty Party were **assassinated** for betraying the tribe. The new Indian arrivals sometimes squabbled with the Old Settlers, the Cherokee who had traveled west between 1818 and 1828.

Finally, in 1846, these groups ended their differences and formed the Cherokee Nation. They were called the Western Cherokee. This name set them apart from the Eastern Cherokee, a small band of Cherokee who had remained in the mountains of Tennessee and North Carolina.

After the Civil War, the government took more land from the Indians to build railroads and establish more white settlements.

The Western Cherokee began to re-create the life that they enjoyed in their homeland. During the 1850s, they had a golden age of success. After the Civil War ended in 1865, however, the U.S. government once again took some of their land. This time the government wanted to make way for the railroads and for more white settlers.

Many American Indians suffered because of U.S. government policies. The Trail of Tears remains the most tragic reminder of the violence and broken promises that the U.S. government used to force Indians off their own land.

GLOSSARY

assassinated—killed for a political reason

attribute—a characteristic of a person or thing

civilized—socially developed

convert—to change from one religion to another

epidemic—severe outbreak of an infectious disease

militia—military force, often made up of local volunteers

plantations—large farms common in the South before the Civil War

shamans—religious leaders and healers of a tribe

stockades—wooden forts used as prisons

DID YOU KNOW?

- In their own language, the Cherokee called themselves Ani'-Yun' wiya, which means the "Principal People."

- As early as 1802, U.S. leaders supported moving the Indians to lands west of the Mississippi River.

- Today, the Cherokee Nation of Oklahoma has more than 165,000 citizens.

- The Cherokee rose is Georgia's state flower. The Cherokee believe that the flower grew wherever a tear fell from a mother's eye as she walked along the Trail of Tears.

IMPORTANT DATES

Timeline

1785	The Cherokee sign the Treaty of Hopewell.
1802	President Thomas Jefferson signs the Georgia Compact.
1828	John Ross is elected principal chief of the Cherokee.
1830	Congress passes the Indian Removal Act.
1832	The U.S. Supreme Court rules in favor of the Cherokee, but President Andrew Jackson refuses to enforce the ruling.
1835	In October, the Cherokee reject the treaty negotiated by the Ridgists with the U.S. government; Major Ridge and his supporters sign the treaty in December.
1838	The Ridgists begin to leave Georgia in January; U.S. troops begin forcing the Cherokee off their lands and into stockades in May; Forced marches to the Indian Territory in Oklahoma begin in June and end in November.
1839	In March, the last of the Cherokee Indians reach what is now the state of Oklahoma.
1846	The Cherokee Nation is formed in Oklahoma.

IMPORTANT PEOPLE

ELIAS BOUDINOT
(1800–1839), *Cherokee publisher and supporter of Major Ridge*

ANDREW JACKSON
(1767–1845), *seventh U.S. president (1829–1837)*

MAJOR RIDGE
(1771–1839), *Cherokee leader who supported the Treaty of New Echota*

JOHN ROSS
(1790–1866), *principal chief of the Cherokee*

WINFIELD SCOTT
(1786–1866), *U.S. general in charge of Indian removal during 1838*

SEQUOYAH
(1760–1843), *creator of the Cherokee written alphabet*

WANT TO KNOW MORE?

At the Library

Brill, Marlene Targ. *The Trail of Tears*. Brookfield, Conn.: Millbrook Press,
1995.

Fremon, David K. *The Trail of Tears*. New York: New Discovery Books, 1994.

Hoig, Stan. *Night of the Cruel Moon*. New York: Facts on File, 1996.

Lowe, Felix C. *John Ross*. Austin, Tex.: Raintree Steck-Vaughn, 1992.

On the Web

For more information on this topic, use FactHound.

1. Go to *www.facthound.com*

2. Type in this book ID: 0756501016

3. Click on the *Fetch It* button.

FactHound will find the best Web sites for you.

Through the Mail

Trail of Tears National Historic Trail

Trail of Tears Association

1100 North University, Suite 133

Little Rock, AR 72207

To get information about the history of the Trail of Tears and efforts
to preserve this historic route

On the Road

New Echota Historic Site

1211 Chatsworth Highway N.E.

Calhoun, GA 30701

706/624-1321

To tour the city that was established as the capital of the Cherokee Nation
in 1825 and to visit the restorations of the Supreme Court building and the
print shop where the *Cherokee Phoenix* was printed

Trail of Tears State Park

429 Moccasin Springs

Jackson, MO 63755

573/334-1711

To follow the route along the Mississippi River—by land and by water—
that the Cherokee traveled on their long march to the Indian Territory

INDEX

About the Author

Michael Burgan is a freelance writer for children and adults. A history graduate of the University of Connecticut, he has written more than thirty fiction and nonfiction children's books for various publishers. For adult audiences, he has written news articles, essays, and plays. Michael Burgan is a recipient of an Edpress Award and belongs to the Society of Children's Book Writers and Illustrators.